Anonymous

Real cookery

Anonymous

Real cookery

ISBN/EAN: 9783744786072

Printed in Europe, USA, Canada, Australia, Japan

Cover: Foto ©Lupo / pixelio.de

More available books at **www.hansebooks.com**

REAL COOKERY.

REAL COOKERY

BY

"GRID"

NEW YORK

CASSELL PUBLISHING COMPANY

104 & 106 FOURTH AVENUE

THE MERSHON COMPANY PRESS,
RAHWAY, N. J.

PREFACE TO THE AMERICAN EDITION.

You must permit me to offer a word of explanation and of apology in inviting your attention to this pamphlet. It is based upon the supposition of no school and no traditions of good cooking. Now these do exist in the great centres from New York to California, and even perfect cooking can be found in places remote from capital towns, in Louisiana, Maryland, and Long Island, because of the tradition having been kept alive through generations. But, alas, " messy " cooking has of late years crept in to an alarming extent, and it is against this that I am warning you; hence, I feel justified in presenting to you an extreme view of the existing state of things, a caricature, perhaps, but still true enough as regards the great majority of Anglo-Saxon feeders.

To you, familiar as you are with the broiler, the grill, and the chafing dish, I need hardly whisper : Do not fry or bake meats ; but I wish to preach simplicity, and to inspire you with the desire of studying this important subject more or less yourself, instead of leaving everything to your excellent and well-paid cook.

As to the variety I urge, it will prove a much easier task for you than for your British cousin, because you have everything he possesses except the sole, and you have an enormous variety besides, unless it be perhaps an occasional canvas-back, or a dish of terrapin that found its way across, the gift of a friend.

The Gaul has the advantage of you in the matter of truffles—I do not admit goose livers, because, if you chose, you could have as good as ever were reared in Alsace; you have only to stuff your bird with Indian corn in the Alsatian fashion, if the Society for the Prevention of Cruelty to Animals would let you.

On the other hand, neither Gaul nor Briton can

boast the glorious variety of food offered by the American Continent—variety so great that *entrées* become comparatively an easy question to solve. I do not feel the need of a made dish, *secundum artem*, if you give me a soft shell crab; and who would want a *salmi* of game, if you give him a grass-plover or a canvas-back? The hard crab in mid-winter is, by the way, a shellfish unapproached by any in Europe, and contains (I mean the female) the richest, sweetest, and most digestible fat I know.

The tiny clam, raw or stewed, is also an advantage you have over your cousins, but it is only in the knowledge of its excellence, because the clam (and the soft clam, too) exist in abundance on the coast of Ireland and Scotland, only the natives would rather starve than eat them.

The only source of danger with you is that you will but too often be tempted to have vegetables or fruit out of season and when not fully matured. I know you do not mind what the cost may be, provided you have a *primeur* to set before your guests, but I maintain a good sound Newtown pippin is better than strawberries tasting of straw.

Your larder is so bounteously filled with good things of all kinds that you may succeed with only a moderate amount of judgment and care on your part in putting a good dinner before your friends, and I hope the very few principles I attempt to lay down may enable you to produce your most excellent victuals in a simple and, notwithstanding the simplicity, in their most succulent form.

ADDITIONS TO AMERICAN BILL OF FARE.

Breakfast.

(Dyspeptics beware of all sorts of hot bread and cakes.)
Hash of all kinds.
Fish balls.
Stewed clams.
Rice cakes.
Buckwheat cakes. } But no syrup.
Hot corn bread.

Dinner.

Besides oysters, Little-neck Clams.
Soups, Chicken with fresh Okra.

Entrées.

Green peppers, stuffed.
  ,, ,, with Tomato Sauce.

Game.

Canvas-back ducks.
Reed-birds.
Rails.
Upland Plover.

CONTENTS.

———✦———

PART I.

CHAPTER I.

CHAPTER II.

CHAPTER III.

CHAPTER VIII.

CHAPTER IX.

CHAPTER X.

CHAPTER XI.

PART II.—RECIPES, *Etc.*

PART I.

PART I.

' I have seen the mahoganies of many men " (THACKERAY, " Mr. Brown's Letters to his Nephew ").

CHAPTER I.

On what Indian cooks call "painted dishes," and on cooks running opposition shops to decorative artists—Dainty meals and real cookery capable of achievement with far less trouble.

IF there is one thing in this world you, my dear reader, and I can cordially agree about, that one thing, assuredly, must be our dinner—the everyday "plain roast and boiled," as well as the average dinner party. The monotony of the former, I know, is as hateful to you as the vulgar richness of the latter. Do you remember Mrs. Smith-

13

Jenkins', the other day, with its pretentious, endless French menu, and the "*saumon en surprise*," consisting of a cupid in rice paste, adorned with rose-coloured horse-shoes, and underneath these a green-dyed *purée* of salmon ? And the "*foie gras*," stuffed into a flock of miniature geese (again in rice paste), these delectable geese floating in a pond of green aspic-jelly ? Why all this masquerade, I ask ? Are we a parcel of children that we require victuals in the shape of toys ? Is it because of the cook's ancient, but silly, privilege to show us they, too, can be painters and sculptors ? No, it is because of our insane desire to dish up everything in some astonishing way—what things taste like matters not. Nor could you expect excellence of flavour when "*dummies*" and garnishes absorb more of the cook's time than the cooking itself.

All this is vanity, humbug, and affectation, if we would only be candid enough to own it. Real cookery—sincere and honest cookery—is quite another thing.

The object I have in view is to explain to

you how, with comparatively little trouble, both your own every-day meal and the magnificent parade of Mrs. Smith-Jenkins could be made pleasant, digestible, and delightful, and it would be easier for me to make myself understood if you will permit me, for the moment, to imagine you slightly dyspeptic, and, therefore, most particular as to the preparation of your food.*

To illustrate the " messy " way we now have of dressing simple things, suppose we take a plain lamb cutlet. It does not matter where you may call for that simple dish, whether hotel, restaurant

* For those who are really dyspeptic, or invalids, I have sketched a bill of fare, with a view to the patient submitting it to his medico. As a rule, the doctor's time being limited, the bills of fare or directions as to diet they give to their patients are equally limited, and, as many classes of sufferers require a varied diet, I would urge all such to get their physicians to look through this bill of fare, amplified by them if they have favourite dishes to insert. I venture to say the medical man could more quickly strike out what is unsuitable than he could write out himself what is fit for his patient. Thus the patient may be tempted to eat, and so to gain strength, by a judiciously varied bill of fare. The cooking in every case must be simple but dainty. (*See page* 77.)

or club, you will be served with a parcel of thin,
bread-crumbed cutlets fried to death, and swimming
in, not a sauce, but a sort of soup, flavoured with
tomato-extract and, possibly, with Peppershire or
similar sauces as well.   If your palate be so
depraved as to make you fancy you enjoy this dish,
your common sense, if not your experience, must
tell you it is very far from the digestible, tasty
cutlet you require, and that the true mode of
serving it is a very different one.   I need not tell
you, an old traveller, that a plain lamb cutlet
(*côtellete d'agneau nature*) means all over France
and the civilised Continent, a moderately thick
juicy cut, carefully grilled over a brisk charcoal
fire, and served with its own gravy only, with a
slice of lemon on a bed of watercresses.   This
brings me to my first three points, discussed in
the next chapter.

CHAPTER II.

No meats to be fried—All sauces, except the natural
gravy, to be served separately—Grilling on charcoal—Eschew gas stoves for cooking of meats, and
do not bake your joints.

My first three points are—firstly, no meats are
to be fried; secondly, they are not to be served
with any gravy or sauce save their own, and
that gravy not diluted to the extent of a soup, any
other sauce being served separately; thirdly, invariably use a charcoal stove for grilling—nothing
better than charcoal for developing the flavour of
meat. This stove costs but a few shillings, and
will often save a coal fire.

No preparing of meats on gas stoves and no
baking of meats to be permitted.

2

CHAPTER III.

On seasoning in the kitchen—Patent sauces not real cookery—Soups and vegetables not to be peppered in the kitchen—Pure wine only, no "cooking" wine—Grilling preferable to frying for fish and fowl, as well as for meat—Caution as to over-cooking.

Do not allow your cook to send up meats unseasoned. Salt and freshly ground black pepper should be judiciously used while cooking, if the flavour of the meat is to be fully developed; but do not, on any account, admit nutmeg, mace, and hot sauces of the Peppershire kind into your kitchen. No condiments to be used, except such as may develop or heighten, none such as are apt to disguise, the natural flavour of each dish, while all peppering of soups and vegetables in the kitchen

18

should be altogether prohibited. If any wine be used, it must be sound, pure, grape-juice out of your own cellar, and not so-called " cooking wine," bought by the cook. It is only too often an adulterated article.

Persuade your cook to substitute the grill for the frying-pan, as to fish and fowl as well as for meat. I am sure both your palate and your digestion will be the gainers by that change.

Caution your cook in regard to overcooking. As a rule, fish and fowl are cooked more than necessary, much to the detriment of flavour and delicacy, not to mention both thereby being rendered tough and indigestible. This remark applies in particular to shell-fish and to the sauces of which shell-fish are the basis. Nothing could be worse than overcooked shrimp or lobster sauce; and many a time, when you thought your fish was not fresh, I am sure it was simply overcooked. (See page 73 for my suggestions as to the preparation of such sauces.)

CHAPTER IV.

On bills of fare and their composition.

Do not expect your cook, unless *more* than usually intelligent, to compose the bills of fare for your daily dinner, or for a party, but do it yourself until, at least, you have properly trained your cook and until you have made her understand your ways. Of course, if the good wife should happen to have a taste for such small matters as cookery, she will do very much better than any one else.

For my own part I would not trust any cook to compose a bill of fare for me. It is an easy task to tell, when you dine out, whether the chef was the sole author, or whether the châtelaine has stamped the menu with her own seal. When six out of eight dishes are truffled, no matter whether the dinner be in January or in July, you may safely back the chef's authorship. And where there is hardly one plain dish, when lobsters, ducklings, &c., appear in the shape of *mousselines* or *soufflées* long odds may be laid on the chef's having had no one to say him nay.

CHAPTER V.

Bills of fare (*continued*)—**Best materials only to be used, including butter and everything that enters your kitchen.**

WHETHER your dinner be for yourself alone or for a party, choose your dishes with an eye to their lightness and digestibility, as well as with a view to careful opposition of colour and flavour, and never attempt to serve a dinner except with the very best materials that can possibly be procured. I do not mean so-called first-class articles, but those of the *highest* degree of excellence. Make it your business to find out where the finest can be had, and, if you be frightened by the price, serve fewer dishes and really first-rate rather than a larger number not quite so good.

When I say " best materials," I mean *everything* that is used for cooking. If it be butter, let it be the best, such as you would yourself eat for breakfast. Your cooking butter cannot be *too good*, because the inferior article is apt to spoil any dish beyond hope, and you would only be " spoiling the ship for a ha'p'orth of tar." Now, this principle applies to *all* materials used in cooking.

CHAPTER VI.

Simplicity, and again simplicity—On the folly of trying to produce dinners on the same lines as the banquets of the rich, who employ first-class French cooks—An excellent dinner quite possible in any house, even in lodgings.

LET your dinner, even for a party, be simple. Really good French cooking is simple and not a bit like the rich, make-believe French dishes we so often meet with, intended to charm the eye by decoration in doubtful taste rather than to rejoice the palate. Allow me also to say to those who are not dyspeptics, but who may be leading indoor lives, that simple, daintily cooked and judiciously varied meats would be far better for their health and comfort than the usual style of cooking at a London dinner party.

24

Do not overrate the capacity and the talents of your excellent, but not highly artistic, cook, by urging imitation of the fancy dishes of the distinguished chef of your most noble friend, the Marquis de Carabas. Depend upon it, with first-class materials, a simple dinner is vastly more successful than an elaborate one. One of the very best dinners I ever enjoyed was given by a bachelor in his lodgings, and the bill of fare consisted only of oysters (no soup), a John Dory, a saddle of mutton, potatoes baked in the ashes, a pheasant, a plum-pudding, and a piece of well-matured Camembert cheese, all washed down with '74 champagne, followed by a grand bottle of claret. In this case perfection had been secured by the care our host had displayed in personally selecting each article, and by the equally careful instructions given by him to the modest cook, or possibly to the landlady herself.

CHAPTER VII.

On *entrées*—the "messy" *entrée*—The too rich *entrée*—
The flabby *entrée*, and why always mashed potatoes
as a basis for the "flabby"?

Of course you require a fuller bill of fare for a
regular dinner party, with soup, ices, and dessert.
You will study to a nicety the oppositions in colour
and in flavour of the dishes, plain though they be.
Each dish then forming a pleasing contrast to the
preceding one and each being first-rate of its kind,
you may rest contented with only one or, at most,
two made dishes or *entrées* as a fillip to your otherwise simple dinner. Being a sensible man, you
will know that your *entrée* should not be a messy,
decorative monstrosity, but a daintily cooked,
digestible dish. Do not attempt to set before

26

your guests such doubly rich and utterly indigestible horrors as a *terrine de foie gras*, covered with a *salade russe* (a vegetable salad drowned in mayonnaise sauce).

Another fashionable and hideously unwholesome dish is *mousse de foie gras*, made of *tinned* goose livers, whipped up with cream. The French way of preparing it is a very different one: *Fresh* goose livers, whipped up with champagne, cooked with fresh truffles and served moulded in aspic jelly. As a matter of fact, the average *pâté*, or *terrine de foie gras* is not a first-rate article, greasy as a rule and containing a good deal of sausage meat. The very finest *pâtés en croute* are, of course, an exception, but you can approach them very nearly by potting fresh goose livers with fresh truffles. Both can be had at Benoist's in Piccadilly.

On the other hand eschew the vapid, flabby style of *entrée*. I mean dishes of the boiled fowl kind, with a flour and milk-cum-nutmeg sauce, or the fried sweetbread floating in an acid, "tomato-extract" soup. I fancy these unsophisticated

attempts at *entrées* have very nearly gone out of
fashion, but they survive in the shape of equally
flabby and tasteless, if more ornamental, dishes
such as *suprême* (breasts) of chicken, adorned with
insipid preserved truffles, or soaking, in the form
of cutlets, around a heap of vapid tinned green
peas, all walled iu by little mounds or a wreath of
mashed potatoes. If the chicken were accompanied
by a dish of fresh, grilled, but not overcooked
mushrooms no larger than a florin, it might find
favour with your guests without costing more.

CHAPTER VIII.

Entrées (continued)—**Good** *entrées* **or none at all—Sauces to be served separately.**

You will readily conclude from the foregoing remarks that your *entrées*, simple though they be, must be more toothsome than the vapid dishes I have named. You will find later on abundant suggestions for *entrées*, but, I should suggest your being content with a good beefsteak and potatoes, rather than striving to produce a dish beyond your powers or simply worthless.

In the matter of sauces let them be served separately. I do not know why the vile habit of drowning every piece of meat in sauce and allowing it to *soak* has penetrated into almost every house. Let your grilled or roasted meat come to table hot and unimpaired in flavour, in its own gravy only; then, if I do not fancy your sauce, I may go without.

CHAPTER IX.

On the importance of taking an interest in cookery, of being on good terms with your cook, and of judicious criticism and praise—On studying the literature of cookery.

I HOPE you have now arrived at the conclusion that you ought not to be above taking a very close interest in cookery. And why, indeed, should you be above doing so? Does not your health depend upon your getting properly cooked and inviting food? Are you one of the favoured few who lead an out-of-door life and who take sufficient exercise to assimilate coarse fare?

And you, dear madam, let me urge *you to* consider the importance of an attractive dinner table if you wish to keep your husband from his club. Be persuaded by me that a small—com·

paratively very small—amount of attention and study will assuredly accomplish success. Do not fear, having once trained your cook in your own sensible ways, that your time and trouble will be lost, for the tradition of good cooking, once established, will survive in your kitchen. Naturally, you and she have become better acquainted through a mutual interest in the art of cookery, and you are, I trust, on excellent terms with one another. You will never withhold praise from her, when praise is due, and you will never criticise her achievements without assigning good reasons for your remarks and without being able to set her on the right track. Do not doubt your ability to do so, for you will be surprised yourself how quickly you will learn, if you use your palate with intelligence, and if you read such works as Sir Henry Thompson's * admirable book on "Food and Feeding," Mr. Theodore Child's† volume, "Delicate

* Sir Henry Thompson, " Food and Feeding." F. Warne and Co. 1891.

† Theodore Child, " Delicate Dining." J. R. Osgood, McIlvaine and Co. 1891.

Dining," and A. Hayward's* "Art of Dining," with Gouffé's classical "Livre de Cuisine," † as a work of reference whenever you happen to be in doubt. But, above all, you must give five minutes to Thackeray's chapter on "Great and Little Dinners" ("Mr. Brown's Letters to his Nephew").

* A. Hayward, "Art of Dining." J. Murray. 1883.

† J. Gouffé, "Le Livre de Cuisine." Hachette and Co. 1888.

CHAPTER X.

On the mistake of employing a French chef if you are not a good judge of cookery—On the well-trained Mary Jane.

IT is not a wise plan for you to engage a superior class of cook, unless you be a good judge yourself. Ten to one he will not be amenable to your wishes, deeming his own judgment superior. He will run riot in all sorts of fancy dishes, *des truffes truffées* will pervade every meal, and he will treat you to high art in the shape of *des pièces montées*, such as you may see depicted in Gouffé. As a sample here is one: a classical vase, contents unknown, capped by a Roman, armour-clad torso (in paste, of course, from a mould *ad hoc*), the said torso flanked by truffles, pierced by swords or skewers. Unless it

3

be the Cupid and horse-shoes (mentioned page 12) could bad taste go further than this? On the other hand, your chef will be for neglecting his sauces, and may even degenerate to the extent of asking for "Peppershire" or other patent sauces, to save himself the trouble of preparing his *sauces mères.*

If you are wise you will be satisfied with a well-trained Mary Jane, not too old to be taught your own ideas and wishes, and you will make a point of going into your kitchen from time to time. I know many ladies do not venture to do so for fear of being turned out by the cook. All I have to say is, that kind of a cook ought to have five minutes' notice to leave the house.

CHAPTER XI.

On the decoration of the table—Again simplicity—No
strong-scented flowers — No "greenery-yallery"
stuffs—Lighting of the table and shades—No fads
or frills—Electric light—Fruit—On menus, and
why always French menus, even for the most simple
and most thoroughly English dinners?—On wines;
here again simplicity and sincerity as to quality.

WHEN you give a modest banquet, judiciously
ordered, you will let the decoration of your table
be as simple as your dinner. No strong-scented
flowers, I hope, and none very expensive. Why
waste your substance on cut flowers? Spend
all you like on excellent food and the best of
wine. I am glad to know you despise "greenery-
yallery" dirty-coloured stuffs disposed limply
on your table, with a flower or two, artfully

stuck into the folds, wherever possible. You seek
all your glory in the finest white napery, bright
silver, glass of the whitest, purest, and finest
shaped, and flowers as nearly as possible of one
pale tint, the leaves being of very light colour.
You have nothing on the table so high as to hide
one guest from the other, and your lights are so
contrived as to light up well the charming faces
gathered around your festive board. You have a
lamp, suspended just above their heads, and candles
on the dinner-table itself, both well screened,
not obscured; but no fads or frills in the shape
of umbrellas or parasols in lieu of shades over
the lights. Only too often have you seen the
frills ending up in a flare. Green or opalescent
shades throw a ghastly hue over every face, and
electric light in the ceiling infallibly casts every
eye into deep shadow. Why, since the introduction of electric light, this mode of lighting a
dinner-table from the ceiling has come into fashion,
must ever remain a mystery. I am sure you are
not as unkind as all this to your fair friends.

There has been, and there is still, much controversy as to fruit being banished from the table. I hope you will weigh that question well, and, whatever you decide finally, I trust you will have *no fruit that is not intended to be eaten.* Any dish of fruit or confectionery on the table solely for the purpose of decoration, is a sin against good taste. Why all this gorgeousness of dessert? Would not one or two dishes of fruit in season serve every purpose? You have given your guests a bounteous feast, surely there is no necessity to pile a quantity of fruit and confectionery on the top of it all.

Since we are at one, so far, and since you mean to be simple, you will not, of course, elaborate your accessories, such as the menu-cards and stands, and, as for the menu itself (which you have succeeded in producing of only reasonable length), as your courage failed you in your attempt to write it in plain English, let the French list of the English dishes produced by your British goddess below stairs, be revised by some well-educated

Frenchman (not by a French chef), else you will be sure to come to grief.*

I am sorry Sir Henry Thompson condemns all attempts at English bills of fare, because, he says, the introduction of certain indispensable French words would result in a " mongrel patois," but, with all deference to Sir Henry's opinion, I hold the " mongrel " to be preferable to the schoolgirl French, frequently misspelt, of most of our French menu achievements.

As a fair sample of these I will select the familiar *œufs de pluvier* (plover's eggs), known to the French only as *œufs de vanneau* (lapwing's eggs). As a matter of fact, the latter are the very eggs we delight in as the plover's; they are the lapwing's or peewit's, belonging to the plover family, but they are not those of the grey or golden plover, which do not nest in this country. I fancy these *œufs de pluvier* would prove something of a conundrum to a French poulterer; but if you, my fair

* Pray save me from menus printed in gold type. Why add to the difficulty of reading small print ?

reader, mean to stick to that word in spite of all, please use the singular and not the plural, also say " sauce à *la* diable " and not " sauce *au* diable."

Why is our honest Southdown almost invariably styled *pré salé* by our intelligent composers of menus ? Surely this is reducing it from the first to the third rank in the mutton world. The French *pré salé* (salt-marsh) mutton cannot compare with our Southdown and, in point of fact, it is quite another article. Perhaps the same intelligent composer would call Severn salmon *saumon du Rhin* ? What I wish to ask now is this : you, with your usual sincerity and good taste, write in your bill of fare tender-loin steaks à *la Rossini*, and a Frenchman, in his, roast-beef à *l'Anglaise;* can either be called a " mongrel patois " ? I hold that culinary terms ought to be entitled to free passes into every language.

Supposing, too, that all our French menus, from the schoolgirl's to the confectioner's or purveyor's of ball suppers, were unobjectionable French, what is the good of them to, say, one-half of your guests, whose knowledge of French, admittedly, is of the slightest ? And as for the hired Robert, do you expect him to be a French scholar and to bring you that dish with a long French name to it ? As like as not he will serve something else instead and will tell you " Hoff, sir."

I am happy to say the fashion of serving many kinds of wine is going out. Sherry, claret, and champagne served together throughout the dinner as well as champagne with the after-dinner wine, are amply sufficient for most people, and doubtless those who indulge in a greater variety will pay the penalty some day. I prefer one wine throughout and that very good, and if I have any doubts as to the quality of the tap, I ask for plain whiskey and soda.

In all things, then, be simple and sincere. Many men besides the writer have urged simplicity. Forty or more years ago one " who had seen the mahoganies of many men " said, " Great folks, if they like you, take no count of your feasts and grand preparations, and can but eat mutton like men."

PART II.

PART II.

You who have done me the kindness to follow me thus far, do not, please, expect a complete treatise on the art of cooking, or a list of recipes, such as the professed cook is in the habit of referring to. My object is only to enlighten you—and any *intelligent* cook—as to good and sound principles. The recipes I give are very few, and are only intended to illustrate these principles, which are :—

 I. Do not fry or bake meats.
 II. Do not cook meat on gas stoves.
 III. Grill whenever you can.
 IV. Do not overcook.
 V. No shams, no "messes," no pretentious efforts.
 VI. Simplicity.

VII. Variety whenever possible.

VIII. Best materials only.

And now we will run through the bill of fare attached to this book and see what suggestions may offer themselves. In every case let your palate and your brains be your best guides.

BREAKFAST.

Bread,

As a rule, is not for the dyspeptic. All but the crust of our home-made bread may fairly be called indigestible. If you do not eat biscuits, try properly made toast. I do not mean the ordinary $\frac{1}{4}$ inch or $\frac{3}{8}$ inch thick piece of sodden bread, simply browned on both sides, lying like a lump in your stomach, but a slice $\frac{1}{16}$ inch thick or thinner, thoroughly toasted through and well *dried*. If it is all crust, as it should be, it will give your teeth three times the work that bread or ordinary toast would give.

Stale bread is best for the purpose,

Tea

If allowed to stand 5 minutes develops tannin, which we know to be most injurious. Make your tea in an earthenware pot, and, after 1 to 2 minutes' drawing, strain off (no leaves, if you please) into the pot it is to be served in. If it has drawn longer than said above, add a pinch of bicarbonate of soda. Avoid taking a great quantity of tea, better have—

Coffee.

Use the best quality only. If you cannot manage to roast your own beans every day, procure freshly roasted, but be sure to grind them in your own kitchen just before preparing the coffee for use. By roasting your own beans you will avoid having an inferior, and possibly an adulterated article palmed off on you; you will thus secure most of the aroma which, in the ground state, is quickly lost to an appreciable extent. Do not attempt to boil your coffee, or to invest in this or that patent machine—none of these are equal to the earthenware percolator. Place in this the freshly ground coffee, 1½ dessert spoonsful for 1 small cup of after-dinner coffee (or coffee extract), pat it down lightly, put a strainer over it, and gently pour through it the *boiling* water. If you be allowed to indulge in this after luncheon and dinner— mind, without cream—you will, for breakfast, add twice the quantity of hot milk or water.

Chocolate.

You cannot possibly get a good article fit for your table at 2 or 3 shillings a pound. As a rule, it is far from being unadulterated with rice-flour, sugar, &c. Better pay a high price for the chocolate, and if you still care to mix it up with rice-flour, &c., then buy that, too, and your purse will not suffer. I use Marquis' *surfin mi-vanille*, costing 10½ francs; the *Kilo* of 2⅕ lbs. (about 4 shillings per pound), and I fancy equally good can be obtained elsewhere in Paris, but not for much less money. For cooking purposes chocolate without sugar (*sans sucre*) is recommended by experienced *confiseurs*. As a beverage I prefer it prepared with water only. Pour very little hot water into the grated chocolate until well mixed; then go on pouring water gradually, and finally let it simmer awhile. If you whisk it to a froth in the cup, you will not wish for milk; on festive occasions only indulge your guests, if not yourself, in a spoonful of whipped cream. I should recommend also your preparing your Cocoa with water only.

Eggs.

By all means have a great variety in your egg dishes. They are all good, whether boiled, poached, scrambled and in omelette form, provided they be soft and provided they be not fried in grease.

Eggs on the plate or shirred
(*œufs sur le plat*).

Put a little butter into an earthenware dish or small pot and cook the eggs no longer than absolutely required to set the white. Serve quickly as they will go on cooking in the pot.

A few peeled shrimps thrown over the eggs *after* cooking are a pleasing addition to this dish, and so are, if you do not mind the expense, oysters. These should be added, with a pinch of cayenne, before taking off the fire; long enough to be warmed through, but not to *cook.*

Scrambled (*or buttered*) Eggs.

Keep stirring the eggs in the previously melted butter, and take them off the fire while still in a liquid state. The usual hard, solid mess is quite unfit to eat. Excellent additions to this dish, or to as lightly cooked an omelette, are peeled shrimps or prawns, crawfish tails and claws, which, being already cooked, must only be warmed up in the dish; also mushrooms, previously cooked, or a thick sauce of beef stock, &c.

Eggs, boiled 3½ minutes, the whites just set and the yolks liquid are excellent, served whole, free from the shells, in a *béchamel* (white stock) sauce with chopped mushrooms, or with peeled shrimps. I prefer this style to the rather flat *œufs à la poulette*, and I do not fancy any preparation of eggs with cheese and cream as being too rich. I much prefer shrimps to prawns, because better flavoured and not so tough as the latter. If you do want a rich dish of eggs, then add to it the shrimp-prawn or crawfish (*écrevisses*) butter, prepared by pounding the shells, &c., and stewing with butter. By the way, why do people persist in speaking of *écrevisses* as crayfish? The crayfish is the clawless lobster (*langouste*).

Hominy.

An American preparation of Indian corn, can be had at the American grocers in Piccadilly. Must be boiled at least $1\frac{1}{2}$ hours. After boiling, grill in little cakes with butter, and season slightly.

DINNER.
Soups.

Diner-out that you are of many years' standing, will you tell me how often you have come across a good plain clear soup, tasting of the meat and vegetables, and not of diluted glue, wine, spices, and hot sauces? The trouble with most of our cooks is that they let the meat simmer too long in the pot by 2 or 3 hours, consequently it tastes of bone, and that gluey flavour has to be disguised by condiments. If you do put vegetables into the soup, I would urge your not sending these to table, but to have fresh vegetables cooked and put into the soup ready to serve, or you may prefer a plain soup with macaroni, vermicelli, Italian paste, custard or what not. If you are not quite fit for solid food, a plain soup with a poached egg in it is excellent.

Use veal and chicken (an old hen is best) liberally for flavouring your soup.

Do not brown your meat intended for soup, and do not colour the soup with caramel.

Shellfish.

That excellent gourmet, Commodore McVickar, of New York, U.S.A., teaches us how to cook a lobster :—

"If you have ever tasted a lobster * boiled in

* I find the same applies to a crab.

my way you will never be so stupid as to buy one ready boiled which, for all you know, may be of yesterday's boiling, if not of the day before. Get a live (green) lobster and put it into a *court-bouillon* of parsley, carrots, a shallot (unless you prefer a touch of garlic), a handful of salt, and a pat of fresh butter. Let the water be absolutely boiling, then boil 15 minutes and add a claret glass of Chablis or Marsala, and allow it to cool in its own *court-bouillon.*"

So far the Commodore, who then goes on to describe the dressing of the lobster salad. For my own part I prefer the lobster served hot in its own *court-bouillon* strained; better still with the latter served in a sauce-boat.

Fifteen minutes is a good average time for boiling, but, as lobsters vary in size, it is well to observe that the fish is done as soon as it begins to float.

Lobster Salad.

If you serve the lobster in the shape of a salad, with lettuce and a little watercress and "mustard," do not, please, kill its flavour by a rich mayonnaise sauce. Be content with oil and vinegar, salt and pepper, and do not let the lobster remain soaking in the mixture, but serve as soon as prepared, not forgetting to add the strained *court-bouillon* to the dressing. I have not the slightest doubt many an indigestion attributed to the much-maligned lobster was due to the mayonnaise sauce in which it probably was slumbering for hours before it came to table, and to other things indigestible, eaten before or after.

I do not hold with those who forbid lobster, not even when my friend is a dyspeptic ; but in that case I recommend him to be careful as to the rest of his menu.

Grilled Lobster.

This is a very popular dish in the United States, and a very innocent one indeed. Again we are dealing, not with the boiled, but with the green lobster, cut in two lengthways.

Now, please, fair madam, do not imagine that

this is a cruel way of killing it. As a matter of fact, the lobsters you buy ready boiled at your fish-monger's are killed in a far less humane way, because a great number of them are put into the pot together, and they linger for many minutes, because the water, though boiling at the moment they are put into it, is chilled at once by the great mass of fish, and I have even heard it asserted that they squeal in their death struggles. Cutting it in two, commencing at the brain, kills the lobster at once, and you may now proceed to put it on the grill, having, of course, washed it well before cutting; add a little butter during the process of grilling. Ten minutes will suffice if, as you ought, you had a hot fire to start with. Some amateurs like the shell burnt to a coal, but I do not quite subscribe to this.

Of course you have cracked the claws and joints before putting on the grill. Serve very hot, with a remoulade sauce, if you wish it. I don't !

Curried Lobster.

Being determined not to use any fishmonger-boiled lobsters, I have none but " green " ones for a curry. Cut up the lobster and stew in its *own juice* and the curry 13 minutes only. Pick the meat from the shells and return to the curry when the latter is sufficiently reduced and ready to serve. If you desire a rich dish, add the lobster butter, as described page 71 (crawfish butter).

The fish thus prepared ought to be exquisitely tender. If you had taken a boiled lobster it would have been hard and dry. Why cook a thing twice ? Shellfish twice boiled—in short, overcooked—must be indigestible.

Baked Lobster.

Stew the green lobster, as above shown, shred the meat and put back into the shells with a little of the *court-bouillon* (see page 51), a few bread crumbs and slightly bake in the oven, salamander. Serve with the lobster butter separately, or with the *sauce diplomate* (see page 71).

Lobster ("G. N.").

One of the best dishes of the French cuisine is the *Homard à l'Américaine* (by the way, not at all an American dish), and there are several very excellent recipes for it. But, to my mind, it is a very inconvenient dish, even if prepared for you alone, because you have to handle the shells floating in a rich sticky sauce. Therefore, I suggest the following modification :—

Having cut it up, stew the green lobster with its juice in a "mirepoix" (see Sauces, page 71), add from half a pint to a pint of good, sound, white wine and half a glassful of brandy. Take out the lobster after 13 minutes, pick out the meat in as large pieces as possible, keep warm in a heated silver dish. When the mirepoix is sufficiently reduced and thickened only, if necessary, with flour or egg, place a boiled head (shell) of lobster upright in the dish and pour over the meat arranged around it the mirepoix, and over that again the lobster butter.

French authorities give 20 to 40 minutes as the

proper time for stewing this fish. My own experience is that 13 to 14 minutes suffice to cook it and I am against cooking any longer than is absolutely necessary.

Crawfish.

These, too, are generally overcooked. Let the *court-bouillon* of aniseed, carrots, and a little white or red wine (or none) be well on the boil before you plunge the fish into the kettle. Have a red-hot poker ready and keep stirring all the time. One minute will do the trick.

They are much better served hot than cold.

The best can be procured at 81, Wigmore Street.

Whitebait.

These are the only fish you are to fry, and you are to pay great attention to the "surprise" of Brillat-Savarin's mode of frying in the very hottest of dripping or oil. Not a particle of grease to adhere to them when served.

Other Fish.

Frying being tabooed, you will readily discover other and excellent ways of preparing fish. Grilled, baked, or *au gratin*, or roasted as suggested by Sir Henry Thompson, or, if simply boiled, then served with plain melted butter and hashed parsley (not " drawn " butter), or with oil and lemon juice, or with a simple *sauce verte* (see page 68). Sir H. Thompson and Mr. Child draw attention to the much-neglected juice of the fish itself. Stew fish in its own *court-bouillon* and serve the latter, strained, but leaving the whole peppers and perhaps a laurel leaf or two in it, garnishing with slices of lemon. The addition of a little thickening and a little white wine will bring you very close to the *sauce au vin blanc*.

Let your grilled fish taste of the fire and serve with a pat or two of *maître d'hôtel* butter, if a bit dry.

Boiled white fish, as most good cooks know, are improved in colour by rubbing with lemon before boiling.

Above all things eschew *purées* of fish or shellfish : they are hateful, and, I think, indigestible to boot.

Many kinds of fish can be dressed *au gratin* in the oven. When you are tired of sole, take a *good-sized* whiting, remove the bones, then a little butter and a squeeze of lemon and a sprinkling of chopped mushrooms and chives will produce a capital result. Cover your fish with buttered paper.

Cold trout and other fish are excellent with a sauce of oil, salt, pepper, and a squeeze of lemon. Finely-chopped chives, too, are a grateful addition to this sauce.

Meat.

In roasting as well as in grilling it is essential that the meat be exposed to a very fierce fire to begin with, in order to set the albumen which then forms a coat in which the juices remain unimpaired ; no knife or fork ought to be put into the meat, because then the juice would escape. For testing steaks or chops a pair of light tongs may be used.

If the meat be spongy to the touch, it is not cooked enough, but as soon as it becomes firm, though not hard, it is done. I have already spoken of the charcoal stove as producing excellent results. It costs a trifle, and a few more shillings will procure a slight wrought-iron stand with rests at various heights, so the grill may be further away from the fire after the first exposure to a fierce heat. If you wish to well develop the flavour you must well brown your steak, chop, or cutlet, the well-cleaned grill, thoroughly heated, having first been rubbed with good butter or dripping, and with onion as well, provided you do not object to a suspicion of its flavour.

The tender-loin, or *filet*, is the tenderest, but the sirloin (*entrecôte*) furnishes the best flavoured steak. A tender rumpsteak, too, is a capital dish.

Steaks.

Serve, only on sending to table, with a pat or two of *maître d'hôtel* butter, placed on top of the steak. (Butter slightly mixed with twice-washed,

finely-cut parsley and a few drops of lemon juice.
Do not fatigue it by too much mixing.)

Cutlets should be cut from the best end of the
neck and they should be thick. Trim neatly and
serve on watercress with a lemon cut into 8 pieces.
Some authorities say a few drops of lemon juice
help the digestion of meat.

Veal is rarely good or tender in this country. If
you must have veal cutlets, have them ¼ inch thick
only after the Viennese style, and serve grilled with
lemon or *maître d'hôtel* butter or with a sharp sauce
of beef stock and pickled gherkins.

Game.

Roasting, whether of meat or of game, is so
thoroughly well understood in this country that I
need only say—roast, don't bake. But the roasting
of wild duck is, to my mind, more carefully done
in America, where a big bird, like the canvas-back,
would have 20 minutes over a very fierce fire, and
a smaller bird, like the widgeon, but 16 minutes.
An excellent bird, the latter, and very juicy, cooked

that way, but it should be served in the American
fashion; that is to say, not carved into thin slices,
but each breast to make one slice, or at most
two (by cutting across, not lengthways). Served in
this way, most of the juice remains in the meat,
and you will not pant for lemon juice and cayenne
to drown the flavour. A salad of tender celery
stalks, cut small, with a dressing of thin mayonnaise is excellent with any wild duck.

Entrées.

I have spoken of meat before touching on *entrées*.
These precede the former at the dinner-table, but
they are not so important a subject; besides the
suggestions already made, there is little left to
describe in the shape of *entrées*. Remember only
my advice—if you have not a " *cordon bleu*," the
simpler they are the better.

Sweetbreads.—l prefer them blanched (cut into
round, flat slices) and *grilled*. If you do not have
the *sauce diplomate*, which is delicious, properly
made, with them, I suggest either grilled mush-

reams or a simple sharp sauce. You may also serve them well stewed in butter and small mushrooms.

Chicken livers.—Stew with a little butter in their own juice and serve with grilled mushrooms.

Cream of Chicken.—Pound the breast in a mortar, pass through a wire sieve, put into a mould with three tablespoonsful of cream and the yolk of an egg, season well and steam 20 minutes. Serve with sweet red peppers, if you can get them, or with lobster, or crawfish butter.

Crawfish claws and tails, picked, with a shell or two between, make a capital garnish.

Chicken stewed with tomatoes and mushrooms.—Small and fresh mushrooms—never preserved ones. Add a little white wine and butter. Do not over-cook the chicken, it must be tender. The sauce must not be a soup. Reduce it sufficiently, and thicken with egg if necessary.

(Preserved mushrooms are hard and indigestible, they taste only of the vinegar they are preserved in, and I say wonder why anybody admits them into his kitchen. I also draw the line at preserved truffles.)

Purées of mushrooms and of truffles are poisonous.

Foie gras (goose liver) should be served in the simplest form, and never when out of season (after the month of April).

Chicken stewed with Celery.—Stew the fowl with celery half an hour, then take it out, and, having previously prepared a sauce with a little butter, celery, and very little flour, mix it with the stock the chicken was stewed in, minus the celery.

Chaudfroids of game birds.

Larks stuffed with forced meat (preferable to minced liver).

Cold Lamb cutlets.—A good neck of lamb, rather underdone, glazed with aspic jelly. Cut into cutlets, and cover each with a mixture of aspic jelly and vegetables, such as carrots, string beans, &c.

Boiled ham and very small *broad beans* instead of the usual spinach.

Vegetables.

None to be peppered in the kitchen except tomatoes, mushrooms, &c.

Potatoes.—Always prefer the mealy to the waxy tuber. If you like them very mealy, put them into cold water, boil up quickly, and give them a good shaking in the pot when done.

If mashed, they must not be a damp, firm paste. No milk or butter to be used.

They are excellent simply passed through a close wire sieve ; and so are potato chips properly prepared, *i.e.*, without a particle of grease sticking to them.

Potatoes boiled or baked in their skins have more flavour than when cooked after peeling.

French (*string*) *beans* should be carefully cleaned ; no strings left adhering. Excellent cold, dressed with oil, vinegar (very little), salt, and pepper.

Cauliflower should be served with Hollandaise sauce (see page 69).

Stewed Cucumber, *Chicory*, *Lettuce*, and *Celery* are improved by a meat-stock sauce.

Green Peas, when really fresh, need only be simply boiled and served with a pat of fresh butter.

Another way, and an excellent one, is *à la Française*, stewed in butter with a little onion or shallot.

Tomatoes, stewed, or cut in two and grilled.

Mushrooms are generally overcooked, and they then loose their delicate flavour. Never have any except perfectly fresh ones with pink gills.

Sir Henry Thompson tells us how to cook giant *Asparagus*. They should be cut of equal lengths and boiled, standing upwards with nearly two inches of the heads out of water, the steam sufficing to cook the heads; boiling 30 or 40 minutes the stalks will be soft and succulent, and the heads will not drop off—only too often the case in the usual way of cooking them. I have found Sir Henry's advice to be most excellent.

Canned *green corn* requires 15 minutes gentle simmering with a little butter and cream. Can be procured at Jackson's, in Piccadilly.

Broad Beans when very small, no bigger than a marrowfat pea, are a most delicious dish, cooked with cream or milk parsley and a little butter. When full size they are coarse, harsh, and they have to be peeled, losing the best part, the skin, which has all the flavour.

Rice with Tomatoes.—Blanch 2 teacupsful of Italian rice, wash in cold water, then 2 tablespoonsful of tomato sauce, a piece of butter, and cover with stock and a little salt. Boil ½ hour.

Rice with grated cheese.—Wash the rice as above, add a piece of glaze, 3 spoonsful of grated cheese, cover with stock, a little salt, and a piece of butter. Boil ½ hour.

While I condemn as a rule things out of season, whether fruit or vegetables (and I must say immature fruit gives very little pleasure or profit to anybody except the greengrocer), while I urge you to have vegetables only when in season, I must confess to a weakness for asparagus in mid-winter. Those sent over from France are very excellent. Well cooked and served on a napkin with a good

Hollandaise sauce, served separately, they make a capital dish after the joint, if you do not mind the expense, though it may not exceed that of some very absurd and highly ornamented *entrée*.

Since vegetables are used largely as garnishes, may I be permitted to enter a protest against the over-elaboration of these into fancy shapes? The latter remind me almost unpleasantly of the necessity of many fingers handling our victuals, and I would rather be without the reminder. After all, not mentioning the wastefulness, it is only a pitiful attempt to charm the eye by the cook's attempts at sculpturesque ornamentation.

I hope you are too sensible and too straight-forward to allow any such shams and any "dummies" whatever to appear at your table.

Sauces.

Of *Sauces* I will endeavour to say as little as possible, since we do not attempt the *grande cuisine* or *cuisine classique*, the sauces of which, as Mr. Theodore Child very justly observes, are

beyond you, unless you possess a very excellent
cook and a good long purse.   But we must discuss
a few besides the very simple ones already mentioned ; those of oil with lemon, salt, and pepper,
and their development, into the *vinaigrette*, the
sauce verte, or the *ravigote*, and we must also say a
word about thickening and glaze.

Glaze is the most important of bases for sauces.
Take thick veal cutlets, reduce with carrots, onions,
and peppercorns, little or no salt ; reduce all day,
strain.   (Can be procured at Benoist's, in Piccadilly.)
Thickening with flour and water, or flour and milk,
or flour and stock should be prepared on the fire,
passed through a tammy, and stirred five minutes
with a wooden spoon while pouring into the sauce.
Thickening with butter and flour (*roux*) is prepared
on a low fire until a light brown, and then poured
into the sauce on a brisk fire until it boils.   Then
put aside, let it simmer 1 hour, and skim.
Thickening with egg is done after the sauce has been
taken off the fire and cooled at least 2 minutes,
otherwise it turns when the eggs are put into it.

Thicken with butter only on taking sauces (or vegetables) off the fire when ready to serve.

Since drawn butter (the French *sauce blanche*) enters so largely into our British bills of fare I may as well state the reason why it is so frequently a failure, tasting oftener like paste than like butter. Gouffé explains—and it may be a sorry comfort for you to know that similar complaints exist in France—that the first reason is the insufficient quantity of butter, the proper proportion being 3 of the former to 1 of flour, and the second the putting all the materials into the pot together, instead of first mixing, with the seasoning, 1 of butter and 1 of flour, stirring with a wooden spoon till boiling, then adding the remaining 2 of butter, taking off the fire and allowing the butter to melt.

Proceed gradually also in making *Sauce Hollandaise.* Mix in the " *bain-marie* " a piece of butter the size of a walnut with the yolk of an egg and seasoning (the germ and the white of the egg carefully removed), keep stirring and take off the fire as soon as the egg begins to set, then add the same quantity of butter, stir until melted, put back on the fire 1 minute, then proceed again with the same quantity of butter, repeating this operation four or five times. When quite thick add a little tarragon vinegar, or, better still, a squeeze of lemon. If the sauce turns, correct by a spoonful of cold water. Some cooks prefer using a whisk to a wooden spoon, but wood is better than metal; therefore, if you use a whisk, let it be a wooden one.

This is Gouffé's recipe, but I have found a much simpler one equally good :—4 yolks of eggs, the juice of 1 lemon, a small ½ lb. of perfectly fresh butter, 2 tablespoonful of cold water ; put all into a saucepan over a brisk fire and whip until it comes to a boil.

Never put *Sauce Hollandaise* into a hot sauce boat, it is sure to turn.

In the matter of seasoning herbs Mr. Theodore Child's remarks deserve every attention, and the allspice described by him, prepared according to Gouffé, is excellent for the—

Mirepoix, which is a basis for brown sauces. Brown in a stew-pan with 3 oz. of butter, 1 lb. of uncooked ham and ½ lb. of fat bacon, all cut into small pieces. Slice 2 onions, 2 carrots, and 2 shallots, and add a couple of bay leaves, a bunch of parsley, and a sprig or two of thyme, also a dozen peppercorns, bruised. Substitute, if you like, the allspice above named for the herbs. When slightly coloured pour in 2 quarts of good veal stock and a bottle of light wine. Boil and strain after simmering 2 hours.

Sauce Diplomate.—Pour into a casserole a quantity (about a pint) of good *béchamel* sauce (white stock), embody with it gradually, and always stirring, just as you do with the *Hollandaise* sauce, about ½ lb. of good butter; finish with a good lump of crawfish or lobster butter, a few drops of anchovy essence, and a pinch of cayenne.

Sauce Soubise is a *purée* of white onions with white stock. Excellent with cutlets.

Crawfish, Shrimp or Lobster Butter.—Pound the shells with all the fat and such meat as may have been left inside of them, and stew with a little butter. The rich fat or butter will rise very soon. I do not recommend your stewing these shells, as some authorities do. Gouffé says 1 hour. I think I get purer flavour by 5 to 10 minutes' stewing than by 1 hour.

" Rough and Ready " Sauces.—A very simple and toothsome sauce is very quickly procurable by frying a shallot with a little butter, adding a little meat glaze, a tablespoonful or two of water, and a little vinegar or a few drops of lemon juice. Excellent with veal cutlets. Another consists of tomatoes and shallots cut up and put into a stewpan with a little butter and parsley and glaze. Pass through a sieve. No thickening required for either of these sauces if properly made.

Use no thickening for any sauce if you can possibly do without. It may give consistency, but rarely adds to the flavour of the sauce.

Sauce Béarnaise.—Whisk ½ lb. of butter with the yolks of 2 eggs, by degrees add a little salt, chopped tarragon, and a spoonful of vinegar.

I cannot leave the subject of sauces without referring to the more than frequent cases of failure of shrimp and lobster sauce. The reason of their pasty taste is that they are, alas, prepared too often with the vilest " drawn butter " instead of with good white stock, and that the shrimps and lobster are over-cooked. *Good* drawn butter, however, with the lobster or shrimps, just warmed and no more, will produce excellent results. I prefer not to flavour with anchovy in case of shrimp sauce ; properly prepared it does not need any extra flavouring. Green lobster, again, makes a much better lobster sauce than the boiled lobster.

Sweets.

Caramel.—One of the best and most nourishing is a rich custard, steamed in a mould lined with caramel (burnt sugar), and flavoured with vanilla pod—not the essence.

Serve with a cream and egg sauce, also flavoured with vanilla.

Chocolate Puffs (*Profiteroles au Chocolat*).—A very light paste of flour and egg that will bake hollow. Cut the puffs in two, fill with rich, vanilla-flavoured custard, and pour firm melted chocolate over the puffs. Serve with whipped cream on a separate dish.

Chocolate Wafer Cake.—Eight or 10 layers of best Carlsbad wafers. Melt, but do not boil, your chocolate with a little butter, mix a portion of it with pounded filberts and spread between the layers. Glaze the cake with the remaining chocolate. Serve with whipped cream on a separate dish.

Chocolate Cake.—Melt 5 cakes or tablets of chocolate with 12 oz. of butter until soft, stir in 12 oz. of sugar, stir in gradually the yolks of 9 eggs, beat up the whites and mix with 7 oz. of bread crumbs ; put into flat buttered tins, bake and cool ½ hour. Ice with chocolate and icing sugar.

Rode Groed (a Danish sweet).—One quart of the juice of equal quantities of raspberries and currants (red) passed through a hair sieve, 4 oz. *German*

semolina and 1 oz. isinglass, 1¼ lb. loaf sugar ; oil
a china mould and boil 10 minutes. Serve cold
with cream.

Mousseline Chocolate Sauce (for farinaceous puddings).—Mix in a stew-pan 4 yolks of eggs, 2 oz. of
butter, 2 oz. of sugar, till thick, add a little potato
flour and the 4 whites whisked stiff, steam 20
minutes, boil 3 tablets of chocolate in syrup for
2 hours and pour over hot.

Ices.

I strongly recommend you to make your own.
A freezer only costs 11s. 6d., and it will soon pay
for itself. You will thus have better flavoured
ices, and you will be sure not to be poisoned.

None of these recipes are, as you can easily see,
very complicated. You will do well by avoiding
any that are.   Let your motto be

" Its own aroma each meat, each vegetable its own
verdure " (LADY MORGAN).

Finally,

Dish up neatly, though not gaudily, and serve hot, very hot, and then you will be sure to please both eye and palate.

PATIENT'S BILL OF FARE.

BREAKFAST.

Bread, home-made.	Biscuits, Captain's.
„ French.	„ Oliver (Bath).
„ wholemeal.	. Unleavened.
„ brown.	„ Oatmeal.
(Should be more or less stale.)	(Toast prepared as on p. 44.)

Tea, prepared as on p. 45.
Coffee, prepared as on p. 45.
Chocolate, preferably water chocolate (see p. 46).
Cocoa, Root's Cuca Cocoa, Van Houten's.
Porridge, boiled at least 40 minutes ; no sugar or syrup.
Hominy, boiled and grilled (see p. 49).
Eggs, boiled not more than three minutes.
    „   poached or as omelette (see p. 47).
    „   buttered with shrimps, ham, &c. (see p. 48).
No fried eggs.
Ham or bacon well grilled and the liquid fat drained off.
Fresh fish preferably boiled or grilled ; none fried.
Kippers, bloaters, Finnan haddocks.

Grilled steak or chop.
Kedgeree.
Cold meat or fowl.

Baked apples.
Marmalade.
Fresh fruit, preferably before the meal.

Number of dishes allowed besides liquids.

LUNCHEON.

Extra dishes besides those on the dinner and breakfast
list :—
    Beef-tea or chicken broth.
        ,,   ,,   cold (in jelly).
With or without pieces of breast of fowl.

    Sweets.
    Savoury.
    Cheese.
    Fresh fruit.

    Cup of black coffee.

Beverages.

Wines.

Alcoholic liquors.

Malt liquors.

Table waters.
Sulis (Bath).
Apollinaris.
Salutaris.
St. Galmier.
Vichy.
Vals.

Number of dishes allowed besides liquids.

DINNER.

No hors-d'œuvres, except perhaps salt sardines or the very best Russian caviar in jars (not in tins), or shrimps (no prawns).

Oysters, the very best only.

Soups, preferably clear soup. No soups containing wine, spices, or hot sauces.

„   chicken or mutton broth.

„   mock turtle, made simply and from calves' heads, light purées (with stock) of celery, artichokes, &c.

„   clear turtle.

No bisques of crawfish (écrevisses) or of lobster.

Fish.

Lobster.
Crab.
Crayfish (langouste).
Crawfish (écrevisses).
No mussels, scollops, periwinkles, &c.
All sorts of salt and fresh water fish except :
Salmon,
Grey mullet,
Herrings,
Mackerel,
Eels, or any fat fish.
Whitebait allowed only if perfectly fresh and served free
from grease ; no other *fried* fish.
Scolloped oysters.
Filleted sole stuffed with oysters.
Sole *au gratin* with mushrooms, tomatoes, and onion.
Whiting *au gratin* (see p. 57).

Entrées.

Calves' heads, plain or with vinaigrette sauce (see p. 68).
Sweetbreads, not fried ; either boiled, stewed, or grilled
(see p. 59).
,,   with *sauce diplomate* (see p. 69).

Chicken breasts stewed in their own juice with a little
>   butter.
>   „   with the addition to the sauce of écrevisse butter
>   and claws.
Cream of chicken (see p. 62).
Chicken coquilles.
>   „   stewed with rice or celery.
>   „   „   „   tomatoes, mushrooms, and a little
>   white wine.
Calves' livers.
Pigeons.
Fowls' livers grilled with or without bacon.
Fowls or game-birds en casserole.
Cutlets sautés.
Curries.
Grilled lobster (see p. 52).
Baked   „   (see p. 54).
No partridge cooked in cabbage, no salonis, no pâtis or
entrées prepared in pastry or pie-crust.

Butcher's Meat.

None fried.
Steak, preferably entricôte (see p. 59).
Chop.
Cutlets (see p. 60).

Cutlets with soubise sauce (purée of onions).
Veal only grilled in ¼ inch slices (see p. 60).
No pork or larded meats.

Fowls.

All sorts, except domestic ducks or geese.

Game Birds.

Plain, roasted, or grilled (see p. 60, for roasting wild ducks).

Game.

Roast venison (not hashed).
       ,,   steak or chop grilled.
Roe deer.
No hare or leveret; rabbit only if very young.

Vegetables.

Farinaceous vegetables, preferably in the shape of purées.
Green vegetables to be perfectly fresh.
No cabbage or egg plant.
Potatoes, preferably passed through a sieve.
Spinach, preferably in purée.
Vegetable marrow.
Cauliflower.
Tomatoes.
Salsifis.
French beans.
Broad beans, only if small and tender (see p. 66).
Green peas, plain or *à la Française.*
Artichokes, Jerusalem.
     ,,   Ball, with vinaigrette sauce.
Mushrooms (fresh ones, not preserved ones), grilled or baked, and not overcooked.
No ceps or truffles.
Asparagus, fresh, not canned.
Macaroni and nouilles, plain or *à l'Italienne* or au gratin.
Cucumber, also stewed, with meat glaze.
Celery, also stewed purée, with meat glaze.
Seakale.
     ,,   cold, with vinaigrette sauce.
Green corn, canned (see p. 65).
     ,,   fresh.
Salad, with plain dressing only (oil and vinegar, salt and pepper).

Sweets.

No pastry of any kind.

All sorts of farinaceous and bread and butter puddings and of stewed fruit with rice, &c.

Riz à l'Impératrice.

  ,, *méringué.*

Sweet omelettes.

       ,,   with rum.

Creams or custards, flavoured with chocolate, coffee vanilla, caramel, &c., but not with any *extracts.*

Jellies, if wine, the best only.

Sponge cake.

      ,,   with chocolate or coffee cream.

Apple or orange fritters.

Pancakes.

Plum pudding.

Chocolate wafer cake (see p. 74).

Baba au rum.

Rode Groed (see p. 74).

Soufflés, light, not sodden.

No ices.

Savouries.

Only simple ones, such as herring roes grilled, bloater, or haddock; no rich, devilled, or highly spiced messes.

Cheese.

Swiss.	Roquefort.	Cheddar.
Brie.	Gorgonzola.	Stilton.
Camembert.	Pont Salut.	Gloucester.

Fresh Fruit.

No canned or candied fruit.

Melon only before the meal.

Apples, grapes, strawberries, blackberries, pears, peaches, raspberries, cherries, oranges, apricots, gooseberries.

Nuts.

Cup of black coffee.

Liqueurs.

Cognac.

Kirsch.

Curaçao.

Chartreuse, yellow.

    ,,   green.

Benedictine.

(For a stimulant, a small liqueur glassful of chartreuse in half a tumbler of water.)

Wines.   Table waters.

                                  Sulis (Bath).

Alcoholic liquor.

Malt liquor.

Apollinaris.
Salutaris.
St. Galmier.
Vichy, Vals.

Number of dishes allowed besides liquids.

www.ingramcontent.com/pod-product-compliance
Lightning Source LLC
Chambersburg PA
CBHW021416090426
42742CB00009B/1165